"I love this book. It is such a helpful, practical teaching tool at just the right length!"

– Robyn Steward, author of
The Independent Woman's Handbook for
Super Safe Living on the Autistic Spectrum

"*Making Friends at Work* is a useful book set out in an innovative and appealing manner for adults on the autism spectrum who are in the workplace. Finding employment when you are on the spectrum can be quite difficult, and once the Aspie, as we call ourselves, has employment, fitting in is the next hurdle. The 'choose your own adventure' style, and the various possibilities indicated by the outcomes on different pages, gives the reader a good idea of what to expect when trying to befriend work colleagues and makes this book a good resource."

– Paul Jordan, author of How to start,
carry on and end conversations

"Planning can be key for autistic people, and this book allows you to plan for potentially difficult situations without falling into the trap of overthinking. Although the subject of making friends is too complicated to be explained in one book, the idea of being able to work through social situations in the comfort of your own home, re-check them and prepare yourself for what could be an awkward interaction is a good one that could be useful to autistic people."

– *Paddy-Joe Moran, author of* Communicating Better with People on the Autism Spectrum: 35 Things You Need to Know

Making
Friends
at Work

of related interest

How to Start, Carry on and End Conversations
Scripts for Social Situations for People
on the Autism Spectrum
Paul Jordan
Foreword by Tony Attwood
ISBN 978 1 78592 245 9
eISBN 978 1 78450 529 5

Parties, Dorms and Social Norms
A Crash Course in Safe Living for Young
Adults on the Autism Spectrum
Lisa M. Meeks and Tracy Loye Masterson with Michelle
Rigler and Emily Quinn
Illustrated by Amy Rutherford
ISBN 978 1 84905 746 2
eISBN 978 1 78450 192 1

60 Social Situations and Discussion Starters to
Help Teens on the Autism Spectrum Deal with
Friendships, Feelings, Conflict and More
Seeing the Big Picture
Lisa A. Timms
ISBN 978 1 84905 862 9
eISBN 978 0 85700 468 0

Social Skills for Teenagers and Adults
with Asperger Syndrome
A Practical Guide to Day-to-Day Life
Nancy J. Patrick
ISBN 978 1 84310 876 4
eISBN 978 1 84642 844 9

Making Friends at Work

Learning to Make Positive Choices in
Social Situations for People with Autism

Saffron Gallup

Jessica Kingsley *Publishers*
London and Philadelphia

First published in 2018
by Jessica Kingsley Publishers
73 Collier Street
London N1 9BE, UK
and
400 Market Street, Suite 400
Philadelphia, PA 19106, USA

www.jkp.com

Library of Congress Cataloging in Publication Data
A CIP catalog record for this book is available from the Library of Congress

British Library Cataloguing in Publication Data
A CIP catalogue record for this book is available from the British Library

ISBN 978 1 78592 375 3
eISBN 978 1 78450 721 3

Printed and bound by CPI Group (UK) Ltd, Croydon, CR0 4YY

Preface

When I was young, I was a big fan of the type of adventure book where you could choose your own ending. What I liked most was that if I wasn't happy with the way things turned out, I could go back and choose an ending that I was more satisfied with. Now, it's not as if I'm ever going to need to escape from an ice palace or out-smart an evil sorcerer in real life, but I enjoyed the process, nevertheless; it made me feel as though I had options, and it made it easier to take risks.

Through my work as a speech and language therapist I have used many resources that support "flexible thinking" and "social interaction," but I wanted to develop something that would allow more autonomy and a broader range of possible outcomes. And so I came back to this idea of the "adventure story" and how it could be used as a tool to explore social interaction.

If you are unfamiliar with such adventure stories, the format is this: after the introduction you are offered a choice of what to do next. The choice that you make influences the path of the story. The story is not sequential like a normal story: you may go forwards or backwards at any point as you pursue a new story line. You will come to an ending sooner or later, which can be positive (you defeat the sorcerer) or negative (you get trapped in the ice palace for ever!).

This book aims to use a similar format to address a social situation. The reader is presented with a scenario (in this case, wanting to make a new friend) and then given choices about what to do next. This will direct the story path. There are a number of endings to this book. The ending may be positive (in this case, you make the first steps in starting a new friendship) or negative (the choices you make don't result in friendship).

Please don't be worried or stressed if you feel the story ended badly; the whole point of this book is to be able to take a step (or more) back and try something else. Perhaps you can then find an ending you are more satisfied with. And if you are curious about what may have happened in some of the less positive endings, turn to the appendix at the back of this book for some possible explanations.

Although this story is based on real life, the outcomes are fictional and as such it should be kept in mind that events will not happen in real life in exactly the same way as they are described in this book. Different people will have different responses on different days and according to their mood. The idea of this book is to explore different choices and outcomes. Feel free to write your own endings based on your own experiences or those of people you know. Maybe you wouldn't choose any of the presented options at all! Talking the choices over with friends/family/key workers/carers will result in a wealth of additional social information. If you want to try things out in real life, you will probably find it helpful to talk over your plans and thoughts with your own circle of support beforehand or afterwards, as a kind of review.

A final note: this story is about a specific area of interest (art). This could easily be replaced by another area of interest if art just isn't your thing (e.g. cinema, sports, graphic novels, music).

There is someone new at work. Her name is Sara. She's friendly: she smiles at me and says "hello" when we pass. I like her clothes and hairstyle, and this makes me think she might like the same kind of things as me. I know she likes art. I like art too and I used to draw at school, but I haven't done it for a really long time. I'm sure she knows a lot more about art than me.

I would like to make friends with Sara but I'm a little unsure what to do next.

Should I...?

Talk to her about art the next time I see her.
Turn to **page 6**

Wait until she talks to me.
Turn to **page 3**

I don't say anything.

"But maybe we could go on Sunday?" Sara says, after a while.

How do I respond?

Say that I could meet Sara at the gallery on Sunday.
Turn to **page 14**

I realise I can't go on Sunday and tell Sara.
Turn to **page 23**

I see Sara in the kitchen one day making a cup of coffee.

Should I...?

Say "hello."
Turn to **page 8**

Wait and see if she says "hello" to me.
Turn to **page 10**

"It looks interesting," says Sara, "and I think it finishes on Sunday."

I say, "Oh, that's a shame."

What should I do next?

Go back to work; I don't think she's interested.

Turn to **page 13**

Ask Sara if she knows what the next exhibition will be.

Turn to **page 12**

"Oh, that's funny," I say, "it's my dad's birthday on Sunday."

"What a coincidence!" states Sara. "I'm having a party at my house on Saturday – you're welcome to come along. There will be a few other people from work there."

"Thanks," I say.

Turn to **page 40**

I see Sara in the kitchen one lunchtime. We say "hello."

"Have you seen the new exhibition at the art gallery?" I ask.

"No," says Sara.

What do I do next?

Nothing. If she wanted to, she would have said something else.

Turn to **page 4**

Ask Sara if she would like to go on Saturday.

Turn to **page 7**

"Do you have plans on Saturday? I'm thinking of going – maybe we could go together?" I say.

"That would be nice, but I'm busy on Saturday," says Sara.

What do I do?

Suggest another day.
Turn to **page 9**

Don't say anything; maybe she doesn't want to go with me.
Turn to **page 2**

I say "hello."

Sara says "hello" back.

"I really need this coffee!" says Sara.

"Oh," I say.

What do I do next?

Tell Sara I like coffee too.

Turn to **page 20**

Tell Sara I don't really like coffee because caffeine is unhealthy.

Turn to **page 16**

"How about next week instead?" I say.

"Well, I think the exhibition finishes on Sunday," says Sara.

"Oh," I say.

"Are you free on Sunday? Maybe we could go then?" says Sara.

Turn to **page 29**

Sara doesn't say "hello." She smiles at me but I feel too shy to smile back.

What should I do?

Leave the kitchen.
Turn to **page 27**

Be brave and say "hello."
Turn to **page 20**

I don't want to miss a chance to meet up with Sara out of work so I say, "I'm having lunch with my dad on Sunday. Maybe we could do something else another time?"

"Of course," says Sara.

What should I do next?

Suggest going to a market next weekend.
Turn to **page 43**

Suggest having tea and cake after work one day.
Turn to **page 31**

"Do you know what the next exhibition will be?" I ask.

"No, I'm not sure," responds Sara.

What should I do next?

Take this as a sign that Sara is not interested in meeting.

Turn to **page 45**

Suggest that I look up the next exhibition.

Turn to **page 21**

I'm about to leave when Nick, who works with us, says to Sara, "I'd love to go to the gallery. Shall we go on Saturday?"

What do I do?

Invite myself too.

Turn to **page 41**

Leave the kitchen: it's rude to invite yourself.

Turn to **page 22**

Sara and I arrange to meet at the gallery at 1pm.

I get to the gallery at 12.55pm. I can't see Sara waiting. I know that people are often late so I wait until 1.15pm. She still hasn't come.

Should I...?

Leave. She must have changed her mind.
Turn to **page 28**

Try to phone her.
Turn to **page 26**

I go back to my desk. I feel twice as stupid because I have no tea and I wasn't brave enough to smile. I think I'll avoid Sara now, as I'm too embarrassed to talk to her.

The End

"You shouldn't drink too much coffee; it's bad for you," I say.

"Oh, I know," says Sara. "I'm just really tired!"

What happens next?

I realise that maybe I said the wrong thing. No one likes to be told off. It seems she knows that too much caffeine isn't healthy.

Turn to **page 17**

I still think drinking coffee isn't good for Sara, even if she is tired.

Turn to **page 18**

I look at Sara to try to work out if she's offended. She is still smiling, thankfully.

"But there are worse things than coffee," I say, and smile back.

Sara laughs. "True!" she says.

Turn to **page 35**

"Oh," I say.

"It's been a long week!" says Sara.

It's been no longer than usual, I think, but I'm not sure if I should say this. So instead I just say, "Yes."

Turn to **page 36**

I go back to get my tea. Sara passes me by the door. She doesn't smile this time.

The End

"Would you like a coffee?" says Sara.

I think for a while. I don't really want one, but it might be a good excuse to continue chatting to Sara.

Turn to **page 37**

"I'll have a look on the website and let you know," I say.

"Great!" replies Sara.

I go back to my desk and look up the exhibition. The next show is not one I'm interested in. I don't like the artist.

What do I do?

Not bother telling Sara because I don't want to go.

Turn to **page 39**

Tell Sara what is on but that I don't want to see it.

Turn to **page 42**

As I leave the kitchen, I hear Sara and Nick making plans to meet on Saturday. It sounds as if they are arranging to have lunch too. I feel lonely. I probably won't go to the art gallery in case I see them there and look as if I have no other friends to go with.

The End

"Ah, that's a shame," says Sara, "but to be honest, it's probably a bad idea for me to make any plans for Sunday. It's my birthday on Saturday and I'm having a party, so who knows how I'll be feeling on Sunday!"

Turn to **page 5**

I phone my dad to cancel meeting him for his birthday lunch. "I'm going to meet my new friend at an art gallery," I say.

"Oh, OK," he says. "I only have my birthday once a year, though."

"Sorry, Dad," I say, and hang up.

Turn to **page 25**

When I get to the art gallery, I tell Sara it's my dad's birthday today.

"Aren't you going to see him?" she asks.

"I was," I say, "but I cancelled lunch with him so that I could come here."

"Oh no, I don't think you should have done that," says Sara.

After an hour at the gallery, Sara says she is going to leave. "Maybe you should go and see your dad? I feel bad that you are here instead."

Sara leaves.

The End

I call Sara. She says she is waiting at the side entrance. She comes to meet me and we go into the gallery together.

The exhibition is amazing and I enjoy spending time with Sara. When we leave, we agree to see the next exhibition together too.

The End

I leave the kitchen without saying anything. I realise I forgot my tea.

Should I...?

Go back to get my tea.
Turn to *page 19*

Leave it there. I might look silly if I go back.
Turn to *page 15*

I go home. I don't feel like seeing the exhibition on my own.

When I get home, I see a text from Sara: "Waiting by the side entrance, are you here? ☺"

I was at the front entrance. I feel embarrassed and text to say sorry. I don't see the exhibition before it finishes.

The End

I have plans to meet my dad for lunch on Sunday.

What should I do?

Go to the exhibition on Saturday without Sara.

Turn to **page 44**

Cancel lunch with my dad.

Turn to **page 24**

Suggest doing something else.

Turn to **page 11**

I don't talk to Sara about the show when I next see her in the kitchen. Sara says "hello" but she doesn't say anything else. I take my tea and leave the kitchen.

The End

Sara says, "That sounds nice. Maybe we can go to the next exhibition at the art gallery?" she adds.

"Yes, I'd like to do that," I agree. "Shall I give you my number so we can arrange a day?"

"Sure. I'll give you a missed call so you have mine too," says Sara.

I text the next day and arrange to have coffee next week after work.

The End

I go to the bar on Friday, arriving at 5.45pm, as I don't want to be too early or too late. Sara is already there and gestures for me to sit next to her. She is also sitting with Michael and we all talk about our days. Alisha, also from work, is going to the bar.

"Would you like a drink?" she asks.

"I'll have a lemonade, please," I say. "Can I get the next one?"

"Sure!" says Alisha.

I think this is going to be a fun night!

The End

I see Sara in the kitchen on Monday.

"I went to the art gallery on Saturday," I say.

"Oh, did you?" says Sara. "I went on Sunday. What did you think?"

Turn to **page 34**

"I thought the exhibition was great!" I say.

"Oh, me too!" says Sara. "I loved it!"

"The next one looks interesting too," I say.

"Yes, I thought so as well. Let's try to go together next time," replies Sara.

We exchange numbers so we can arrange to meet when the next exhibition opens.

The End

"Speaking of worse things than caffeine," she says, "has anyone told you about drinks after work on Friday?"

They haven't. No one ever tells me about going out after work.

"Not yet," I say.

"Oh! Well, we're going to the bar just down the road from about 5.30pm. You should come!"

"Thanks," I say.

Turn to **page 32**

Sara picks up her coffee. "OK, have a good day, then," she says.

"Thanks," I say.

Sara leaves the staffroom. I think I missed a chance to talk to her.

The End

"Yes, please," I say.

"How do you like it?"

"Just black, please," I reply.

"Here you go," says Sara.

"You know, if you like coffee, there's a great place near here," I say.

"Oh, really? I don't drink a lot of coffee, but I'd like to go and get a break from this place!"

Turn to **page 38**

I hope I am not being too forward but I say, "How about tomorrow?"

"Great!' says Sara. "Meet you outside at 12.15pm?"

"Sounds good. See you then!" I say.

I look forward to chatting some more over a cup of coffee (or tea!) tomorrow.

The End

I don't let Sara know. A week later I see her in the kitchen. "Did you find out about the exhibition?" she asks.

"Yes, but I didn't want to go," I reply.

"I thought you were going to let me know," says Sara.

"Well, I didn't really want to go," was my response.

"Oh, all right. Have a good day," says Sara, and leaves the staffroom.

The End

I pluck up the courage and go to Sara's house party on Saturday night. There are two other people I know from work there, and we chat about our days.

"Thanks for coming," Sara says when I leave, "and let's see some art soon!"

"Yes, let's!" I say, and happily head home.

The End

"Would you mind if I join you?" I ask.

Sara and Nick look at each other. I wonder what they're thinking.

"Of course not!" says Sara.

"The more the merrier!" says Nick.

I think maybe I will make two new friends now, not just one.

The End

I'm a little worried that Sara will think I'm being negative, or that I don't really like art at all. Or maybe the new exhibition is by one of her favourite artists and I'll offend her by saying I don't like it. But when I see her next, I tell her what I think.

"Never mind," says Sara. "It's not everyone's cup of tea! People don't always like the same things, especially when it comes to art."

We agree to go to the next exhibition...if it's something we both like!

The End

Sara says she likes that market. I would like a new top and so I ask Sara if she would help me choose.

"Of course!" says Sara.

I make a plan to meet her next Sunday instead and we have a great time at the market.

The End

I go to see the exhibition at the art gallery on my own. It's really inspiring.

What do I do?

Tell Sara what I thought when I see her at work.

Turn to **page 33**

Say nothing. I don't think she really wanted to go with me anyway.

Turn to **page 30**

I think that Sara isn't really interested in talking to me – surely she would have said more if she was. I take my tea and go back to my work. I go to see the next exhibition at the art gallery, but I go on my own.

The End

Appendix

What might have gone wrong? Why did the story end here?

Page 15   Initiating

Sometimes we need to make ourselves be brave and do things that might feel difficult. In this case, a smile and a glance, or even a greeting, would have looked friendly and might have led to a conversation. You could have made a joke of the situation if you felt awkward, saying something like "Silly me, I left my tea behind!"

Page 19   Non-verbal signals

Sara isn't being especially friendly, but she isn't being unfriendly either. And that's OK. You gave signals (by not speaking and leaving the room) that you were not particularly interested in being friends. Trying to make friends takes a bit more effort than smiling to move things forward – for example, saying "Hi" or "How are you today?"

Page 22   Communication repair

By walking out of the room and leaving the conversation, it probably seemed as though you weren't interested in doing something together. To invite yourself without appearing too direct, you could say, "Would you mind if I join you? I'd love to see the exhibition too."

Page 25   Social expectations

Sara probably feels awkward at the end of this story. She is likely to feel bad that you are seeing her instead of your dad on his birthday, which is quite an important day (this might have hurt his feelings too). You could have fixed this by finding another day to meet Sara so that you wouldn't have had to cancel plans to meet your dad.

Page 28 Making mistakes

Give people a chance, and don't worry too much about making mistakes – they happen to everyone! You could have given it more time, or checked where Sara was by phoning or messaging her (you could say something like "I'm here but I can't seem to find you. Whereabouts are you?"). It was a mistake, but not a big problem, so no need to be embarrassed for long!

Page 30 Maintaining relationships

Sara would have been expecting you to say something. Because you didn't, she is likely to think that you are not really interested. She is not likely to say anything more as she won't want to appear keen to be friends when you don't seem to want to be friends with her.

Page 36 Things in common

This was probably taken as a rather unfriendly response. People often don't like to hear a different opinion to theirs when first getting to know someone, whether the opinion is based on fact or not! They prefer to find things that they have in common. If you wanted to appear more friendly, you could try to understand things from Sara's point of view.

Page 39   Apologising

You probably looked a little unfriendly! You said you would have a look at what was on and this implies letting Sara know too. Saying that you didn't want to go sounds as if you didn't want to go with Sara. To fix this, you could apologise for not letting her know, and suggest going another time or doing something else instead.

Page 45   Persevering

There are a number of reasons why Sara didn't say more. She might not have realised that you were thinking about asking her to go. She might have been tired or thinking about something else. She might be shy too! Next time, you could say something like "I was thinking of going, do you fancy joining me?"